# BECAUSE WE SING

# WITH THE EARTH

# VOLUME II

*COLLECTED POEMS*
*OF*
*PENNY HEMANS*

2016

First Edition

Printed and Published by
Leiston Press
Unit 1 - 1b Masterlord Ind Estate
Leiston
Suffolk
IP16 4JD
01728 833003
www.leistonpress.com

ISBN: 978-1-911311-04-1

## BATS

*Long days*
*Quiet nights*
*Hushèd bosoms*
*Beaten brows*
*Milkèd cows*
*Back to base*
*Chased home*
*By lingering moonlight*
*And bats' shadows*
*Panning across*
*Night clouds*

# CONTENTS

# HOGMANAY 1971/72

It was too cold for bats at midnight, even the moon had gone
To bed, but I hadn't!  Waiting, the grandfather clock ticked
The Old year into the New, then came a knock, rat a tat a tat,
On my front door, and there stood Henry!  Holding in his hands
One lump of coal and one slice of 'tin' bread.  Of course, I
Entered into five minutes of hysteria, hugging my friend
And holding him tight, our bodies locked in a frenetic
Embrace.
"What sort of welcome is this" he jested, raising his hand
to his empty lips.
Inside, my living-room was filled with warmth from the log fire.
We filled our glasses with rich champagne
Sharing the gift of friendship
At half past midnight on 1st January 1972.
At half past midday on 1st January 1972,
My girlfriend, Freda, mockingly remarked
"What were you doing with that man last night!
You know he's one of them!  Did you, you know,
Did you do it?"
I shook my head at her in disgust and walked off
Remembering the happiness of sharing an innocent communion
With one they called "Nancy Boy".

I was glad he had been there to celebrate Hogmanay with me
Because we were mates and I would rather have his friendship
Than anybody else who dares to question who or who I should not
Share my time with
I think they should unplug their mouldy brains before
Criticising someone who's never hurt a fly
*dedicated to Henry, a man in a million*

## CHILDREN ON HOLIDAY

There is a hush tonight
while the children's voices
are thankfully quelled
by fractious parents longing for an evening's peace
"Shush up you bawheeds! You've had your story
now go to sleep!"
I hear them
lingering at doorways, loving eyes
exhausted minds, longing for respite
from the energy of fledglings on vacation
then - blissful cessation of their youngest's urgent screams
as he falls into restless dreaming

*August 1984*

~**~

## WISHING

playing with the child upon the grass
I remembered my own childhood
wishing I were there again
but plucked from me too soon
too soon

*September 1984*

## JOURNEY WITH MY UNCLE-IN-LAW

joined my Suffolk uncle
in his caravan
to Langholm hills;
drunken uncle
in his pink-striped boxers
drove me out by
strident midnight snoring;
slept on cold stone floor
in the ladies' loos,
while owls
sang hooted serenades;
backache, frozen shoulders, head aflame,
I caught the morning bus
back home again

*May 1985*


## DESIRE

why do you have no desire within you
why do your eyes glaze like opal drops
when you see my nakedness
what did she do to you
to make you so cold

*August 1989*

**GOSSIP** : *(on hearing Martin Luther King's speech "I have a dream")*

Like you, Martin,
I too have a dream
it does not take much -
I have a dream
to see perfection in my human encounters
to steal away from hatred
to become pure
not to treatise on mind and disgrace -
gossip is a destructive force
I have a dream
to feel as I feel Love
to see as I see the passing of the seasons
to smell the sweet scent of lavender
to taste life's rich endeavours
to rule out heartache and pain -
do not waste me on your bitter tongues
why do you discuss me so?
am I that colourful?
do I inspire your tittle-tattle
to chitchat and laugh at my sadness?
or can you not recognise the real truth
that happiness swells within my soul
and I am laughing with my God
who knows -
wonderment is His offering
you have lost and I sorrow for you -
one day, the rumourmongers shall discover
that we are all the same
not as dirty words on playful lips
but as bounteous spirits
leaping upwards and blending into
oblivion

**THIN SKIN, OR THICK?** *(a bad experience)*

My pants are on fire
the Fireman says
'Don't panic!'
but
my pants are on fire!
the Fireman asks
'have you thin skin?
or is it thick?'
offended
I pour water
on my cellulite burns
while a voice
in the background
argues
'she'll be right mate!
thick-skinned Madonnas
don't hurt that easy!'
I shall never trust
an Australian fire-fighter
ever again
especially if they
come from Sydney

*Sydney, 1985, after an episode with a chip pan filled with hot fat*
*ps: they're pretty darned good really, the Ozzie firemen - and gorgeous with it!*

## A WALK ON SNETTISHAM BEACH 1989

Today we were walking tall
While the flying birds
Swept windward
Against those darkening clouds
And I felt at peace
Because you had taken me to my Heaven
Then you said, out of the blue
'Don't hassle me!
There is always another who can take your place!'
Such insensitive words from a man who thinks he is complete?
How can you say 'do not cause me any grief.. or else!'
Are you so perfect?
Perhaps if I were twenty again
You would love me as I was then
I think you would
And now?
After time has painted on the greys and golds
The tide washes in new lines and memories
And with each ebb and flow
We grow closer
I shall try and understand you
You have placed closure on your heart from your past experiences
I have a book on Freud
Maybe you will find the answer you are seeking
But don't blame me if your sharp tongue
Belies the impotence you are trying to hide
If I cannot help you
Then I shall move on
Like the migrant whimbrels feeding here
On the shore of Snettisham Beach

## ON MEETING BRUCE PEARSON AT WELNEY

As the Whooper Swans flew in formation
and scudded on the surface of the marshy mere
I felt a joy within
my cold spirit
lifted from the friendship given
a helping hand
a smile
a watchful eye
his handsome face so full of mystery
I longed to hold him
and to say 'hello'
his beauty
his art
all emanating from within
all embracing
and I perceive within my memory
glimpses of an artist brushing colours
onto canvas
his tartan shirt
making my heart jump
breathtaking
an inspiration -
as were his pictures of the white birds in flight
while the image of Sir Peter Scott
smiled out at us from his photograph
hung high in the hide at Welney

*circa 1989/1990*

**E282**

I'm beginning to laugh at the pain
I feel
The steam roller
Crushing
Rolling
Bruising
Funny how she flies through my channels
And does not switch off
Nor counter-current like an AC/DC
On on on in constant motion
As though I should submit!
Negative
I put my mind to positive thought
Telling the pain "I quite like you"
There is a slight cessation
A dampening of the pain's invasion
Oh bother
It has come back again

*October 1990*

## VALENTINE'S DAY 1991

Waiting for the drop of a letter onto the mat
I worked busily
watching the outside world for a human shape
I turned to more mundane tasks
then saw the shadow pass my window
his bicycle bent beneath a heavy load
they did not feel my tears
nor see the cry of unloved years
without a Valentine
treading over empty floors
banging the warped door wet from snow
gingerly walking icy pavements
upwards towards the hilltop
Ted the local tramp
stopped me briefly and remarked
"You's moind yer seat now else you'se'll fall!"
smiling blackened teeth through bristled beard
such a pitiful fellow
all bandy legged with pauper destiny
then, harping at his wizened face
I scoffed at him "Not I!"
but in a moment's breath
the ice jumped up to meet me
WHACK!
bruised-blue fingers, mottled ebonies on wounded skin
steered painfully to college
following the slushy tracks of forward vehicles
and – thinking of a man who once I loved
who saw the truth of reality

I wondered -
perhaps he could see my past
 those sultry days
when love was with me –
and now?
what future visions did I perceive?
only shadowed walls and drifting clouds
dark was the dusky trail after the day
my tortured heart increased its beating
as shaking hands felt the Yale lock give to emptiness
crestfallen I slammed the peeling door
and climbed the stairs to bed

*Wickham Market, 1991 : one of the loneliest days of my life*

## IN THE APPLE ORCHARD AT TERRINGTON ST CLEMENT

'Our Father, Who Art in Heaven'
came to my mind
surfaced and sang
while I picked apples
so
I wondered
'Who is calling for me?'
my daughter
my son
my lover
my father
my mother
my sister?
who needs to tell me they are alone?
maybe it was just my conscience
imbibing a little religion
into my memory

*September 1991*

**HAPPINESS - PACKING APPLES AT TERRINGTON ST CLEMENT**

The three ladies
And I
Clothed in faded aprons
Laundered
To remove the apple stains
Packing freshly picked fruit
Heaving boxes
Singing songs
Bagging 'sixties'
Watching the boy play on the resident rusty tractor
As though he were the Star of Bethlehem
I ask
'Do you read Rupert Bear?'
Such a stupid question!
He grins wickedly
Benjie with the happy face
Ignores my maternal gaze
And continues his game
This cheeky Piscean with the catching smile
Stay awhile

*September 1991*

**ALWAYS GOODBYE**

I said farewell
to my Capricorn friend yesterday
Paul with the handsome face
who I shared many happy moments with
picking Plums at Terrington
and laughing at the purple stains
on happy lips
after tasting the fruits of our labours
our arms closed around each other
in friendship
briefly
yet another era completed
I am always saying
goodbye

*October 1991*

## KARMIC CONTEMPLATION

What are you doing to me
The man I call the Cobbler
Hob Shoe Hob
The man with the shoe monger's name
When you called today
You sounded dejected in your solitude
Yet all you are doing
Is learning life's lessons
Same as I, me,
Contrary Mary
Heckling the Little Maids
As I ponder under duress
The hours of contemplation
Wondering whether I should live or should I die
Only the pictures of my children
Keeping me sane within my loneliness
Why do you ring me
Hob Shoe Hob
Has your new lady rejected you
As you rejected me
Is your karma catching you
Like-minded we two
Our paths in parallel
We cannot turn our heads
Without it bouncing back with its reminder

*March 1992*

## DARK SKIES OVER DUBLIN
*(a song written for an Irish lass – college – 1992)*

**Chorus:**
*Dark skies over Dublin*
*.Rainbows over Crewe*
*Colouring my senses*
*Embellishing in pictures*
*My visions of you, yes, my visions of you*

When I hit the road
I'm a traveller once more
Seeking a free life
Golden treasures in store
Then I see your face
Such incredible grace
An' I ask myself
"Who am I?
 Can't think why
 What's the reason I'm doing this for?"

So I search for the answer
In stream, shore and sea
I know I'm a man
Who longs to be free
But when I grow old
My soul I'll have sold
If I stay
Make me pay
For the pleasures I sought will haunt me

Lord don't toll those bells
Don't give up on me now
Sweet Cherie, I'm returning
To honour my vow
For the love in my heart
Knows we never should part
Wait for me
Patiently
Till the mountains are covered with snow

The road has no end
The fields are all green
My journey's a long one
My body's so lean
From the long lonely miles
Mixed with wandering smiles
Soon I'll be
Home with thee
And I'll sing you the sights I have seen

**Chorus :**

*Dark skies over Dublin*
*Rainbows over Crewe*
*Colouring my senses*
*Embellishing in pictures*
*My visions of you, yes, my visions of you*

# SONG (A Duet)

Both: Why do the flowers bloom so fair
            Why are your eyes so blue?
    Why do you say our love has died
            Why do I turn from you
            O why do I turn from you

Mary: Take me away to the distant shore
    Where the Green Hills shine with light
    For there you said that you'd be mine
            Loving you was O so right
            Yes – loving you was O so right

Lad: O Mary Mary can't you see
            I've many a mile to roam
    For I'm a wanderin' Irish boy
            With dreams so far from home
            Aye – with dreams so far from home

Mary: Then I shall kiss thee one more time
            To speed you on your way
    And maybe soon you'll realise
            This lass was here to stay
            Yes – this lass was here to stay

Lad: There is no lass as sweet as you
            My Mary of the Vale
    There is no one who was so true
            Yet now I must set sail
            In truth, yet now I must set sail

Both: Why do the flowers bloom so fair
            Why are your eyes so blue?
    Why do you say our love had died
            Why do I turn from you
            O why do I turn from you

*written for a fellow student at podiatry college, a singer with her band, November 1992*

## JAMIE

I read a story about a little boy today
So sad that God took his soul away
So soon
Before he had time
To know the world

I wrote this song for you

Song… dedicated to the Jamie Gilmour fund

City of calm
City of charm
You hold me
You enfold me
When will you tell me your secret
You took my baby
Wrapped her in your velvet glove
Shined her shoes and brushed her hair
What do I care?
What do I care!
Is she there
Waiting for me, waiting for me?
Guess I'll keep on walking
Till I feel her pull at my shirtsleeves
Oh baby's been taken by the
City of calm
City of charm
How you hold me
How you enfold me
City … …

*Dereham, Norfolk, mid-1990's*

## THE VOICE OF DESTRUCTION

The soliloquy of Nations
ratbeats a timbre on a discordant orchestra
their fragile strings
resonating in fits of misery
while puppets gather -
a tragedy of sunken faces
staring silently, waiting
discern a distant rumble
echo across the pitted landscape
dust clouds, an epitaph in slow motion
drift on the explosion's wake
depositing handfuls of gruesome flesh
so nearly, oh so nearly
a thumping, beating substance of humanity
and following behind
a stillness that only despair can understand

*After Diana's speech on land mines*
*The images of the wounded children haunt us to this day*

## THE ANGEL

In England's soil an angel lies
Soft breath adding to dampening dew
Her eyes search upward, scouring heaving skies
So laden with the sadness of a human crew
Dark eyes of the dead linger silently
Clawed hands reaching out to feel
Our new-born angel whose heart burns fire
Indeed, no satanic creature this warm heart may steal
Golden her hair, her lips so white
Closed against a sonata of mirrored pearls that gleam
She it is who has the angel's right
To leave behind a legacy, a dream
The tortured huntress in her hour of joy
Entered a kingdom where her heart could beat
Quietly, at last, within a momentary glow
Such pleasure was for her a transient heat
And as the soil grows cold in autumn's reign
Thus does her mantle close about her soul
Drawing her ever further, her soul from pain
Leading her to an everlasting Heavenly goal

9 September 1997
Sent to Earl Spencer in memory of Diana

## ALZHEIMERS - AN OLD SOLDIER

(Major A T Hemans – November 1997)

The old man sitting in his fireside chair
His left arm swollen and resting in a sling
Looks up with vacant eyes
He shows no element of surprise
When I walk in
   His toothless smile when sensing someone near
Showers me with girlish memories and then
Laughing, he speaks my name
"Pen-Wen, is that you?"
And so begins the game
   "You are old Father William, the young man said!"
He lives in a far off Wonderland and more
And while I listen to his countless odes
Recalled from heady, infant modes
I view the child he was before

A sudden shriek of fright bursts from his cracking lips
I see his craggy face screw up in pain
As in haste he knocks his broken arm
Against a wooden frame, then shouts
 "The spider has returned again!"
It takes some time to soothe his troubled mind
"I have a job for you to do" he flares
"We have to catch the blasted creature unawares!"
So down on my knees, I eventually find
Two woodlice hiding underneath the stairs

A momentary lapse of caution brings my tears
Remembering all those happy years
When we were free of all this sorrow
Looking forward to a new tomorrow
And all we are left with now are relentless fears
   Four hours pass and I watch his sleeping form  -  his mouth wide open ,
His head retracted in an ungainly state
And as the sun sends forth a dusky glow
Through the front door walks a lady - well I know –
My Mother has returned, and I stand up and wait
   With guilt I kiss her tenderly and welcome her inside
Happy that soon I shall be free of care
Thankful that it is not I who has to shave
My Dad and wash him "under there!"
I close the door behind me with a daughter's merry wave
   A once-proud Major in the Yeomanry corps
Has lost his dignity
Perhaps a little more than others past his prime
Yet thankfully he does not seem to be aware
Standing to attention when old friends come to share
His time, his salute is as fine as the young recruit
Tho' his uniform be stained with emissions of incontinence
He is happy, all in all
When his comrades come to call

## POEM FOR COSTA

Darling
I have just touched the hand
of the Poet Laureate
Or rather - he touched my soul
Because he reminded me of you
Silently I listened to his prose
As I sat two chairs distanced
The only solitary figure
In a sea of faces
And twice he saw me
Twice he acknowledged my existence
And something told me
That I must begin to write again
Because I have felt the energies
Of a living genius
While my higher self expressed her desire
To commit to paper
The wonders of my meeting
With a man who stole my heart away
Could it have been only two years since?
No
It has been two, three, four lifetimes...
And as I live and breathe
Yet will I cherish him...
Thank you to the universal law of recognition
For bringing my reality back to me
For stirring the cinders of my mind
And reigniting the fire of creative memories

*Terceira, November 1997*

## SAYING I LOVE YOU AGAIN

Costa meu amor
It isn't only the sensation of
complete bliss
when I am immersed in your arms -
it's the way you look at me
with those big brown eyes
that shine
Sweet love of mine
It is the way you say
'I Love You
Penny Helen'

*Lisbon, December 1997*


## GOODBYE TO MY FATHER

What do you say
when you see your father dying
when do you prepare yourself
why did he have to suffer
a man who had given only goodness to the world
I sit beside you, Dad, and hold your hand
then you try and whisper something
through a guttural, primal sound
so I reach over and stroke your brow
saying "It's okay Dad.  Mum will be alright!"
and with an imperceptible motion
you relax and fall swiftly into your own night
"Goodbye my belovèd Father"
your breathing changes and suddenly
        you are gone

*St George's Day, 1998*

# TRIBUTE TO THEO

*(Dad's cousin, married to Jack Raine, the Hollywood actor who played film parts such as Dr Watson in the 1930's)*

Theo was a lady of the morning
As the waking day was serenaded by the chorus of the dawn
You would hear her softly sing
And harmonise with the sweet melody of the nightingale
Calling for his mate as Theo would call for hers
His eyes watching her through ochred oils
High on the mantelpiece -
Theo was a lady of the middle day
Immaculate and charming
Her radiant smile touched the hearts of those
Who chanced to pass her by -
Theo was a lady of the evening
Her grace and vivid beauty shone
As she shared a waltz with her beloved Jack
Such pleasure for her
This was her contentment -
Theo was a lady of the night
Her autumn years were filled with memories
Of joyful days in California
Mingled with the heady presence of the Suffolk air
And now? Now she has departed
Leaving not with a heavy heart
But with a smile she shared with me
During those final moments of her living breath -
we shall remember that with grace she joined us
And with grace - She has left behind  A gentle memory  -  Of a lady with
auburn hair

*15 February 2000*

24

**GREY WOLF** *(a Native American Chieftain from Southern Colorado)*

Grey Wolf
leapt into my dreams
and there he lingers
quiescent through sultry days
always my guide
and all I ask
as one small gift from you
please stay
may your essence
pulsate in a tender rhapsody
as we journey through this lifetime:
thank you Great Chief
for giving me clarity of mind
for bringing me joy
and most of all
for your constancy
Grey Wolf with the heart of steel

*Boulder, Colorado, April 2001*


**CIRCLES** *(after being treated by three gifted healers in Boulder, Colorado)*

The deepest wisdom
Showered upon my soul
Altered my structure
Integrated this knowledge
With my physical form
So burdened from a leaden heart, then
Lightened by hands of magic
All six together
I felt the cessation of pain
Thus, on my departure from these tender beings
I carried with me
Exquisite memories – and hope
That this was not the end
But a rebirth
And an enduring grace of friendship

*May 2001*

## NANCY

I was reading a title in the Boulder Library called
"Older Than Rain"
A book about the Rocky Mountains
An epistle to those Great Spirits
Whose tortured peaks fragment striated clouds
Between shards of mesmerising Colorado sunlight
Then I heard that you, Dearest Nancy,
Had left us behind
Moved on
And once met by Hubert, Dad, Stuart, Valerie and Theo
You blended with their spirits
And became One with the Universe
At peace
Yet still laughing as you always do
Saying to us all down here
"Why Darling, it is good to see you!"
Nancy, we shall remember you
Not as a sweet, tremulous old lady
But as a huge, generous, multi-talented personality
Whose charm lives on
Go well
We miss you
Just as the world misses your laughter
And the gracious way you entranced us with
Your stories of your Debutante days
In the London of the 1930's

*Boulder, Colorado, May 2001*

## A SOUL'S EMBRACE

When the panther prowls
Shadowed by the dusk before the moon rises
Over the guardians of his terrain
He calls to claim his right to freedom, then
Eyes bright
They pierce the gloom
Lock onto the solitary image of Grey Wolf
Whose dauntless spirit entered my sorry soul
Flooded my emotions with an intensity so profound
That in one micro-second
I knew I had met my match
The one who I had 'seen'
Before the mountain's embrace
There is an unwritten, unspoken code that reads
"This is how it should be"
Love on a magic carpet
Woven to catch our dreams
And spit out nightmares which bombard vulnerable minds
The strength of the Dream Catcher
Our eternal flame
The Panther submits
Slinks off and blends with the night
While Grey Wolf curls into a ball and sleeps
Waiting for a tender hand
I wait
Content within my vacuum
Until you come to me

*dedicated to John and Allison Cardarelli,*
*Eden, Boulder, USA...*

## FASCINATION

I saw the dancer
naked
I watched with fascination
Peter Greenaway's production of
'Prospero's Books'
and as Caliban danced
totally uninhibited
portraying genitalia
perfect in their form
I remembered
when I could share
the sexual pleasure
the exquisite delight
of being loved
long ago
I search my body
and wonder
am I past the age
to dabble in desire?
I cannot believe
a man's loving touch
is lost to me for ever

*November 2001*

## SUFFOLK

*(a dedication to our brave warriors who left us the legacy of Suffolk as it is today)*

Gravelled amber on Aldeburgh beaches
the Barn Owl hunts over Orford reaches
Thespians tread the boards at Friston
while harpsichords in Barnadiston
join the peal of leaden bells
whose sonorous tones blend with the swells
of storm flung waves which crash and moan
and die on Shingle Street alone
the rotting roots of forest pines
grab at the unsuspecting lines
of booted piéds in strict formation
walking the tracks of conservation
but the Eagle Guardian at Henham Lakes
reminds us all of Suffolk Wakes –
        1914-1918 and 1939-1945

*November 2001*

## HAJEMEMASHITE

When the common man plays the tune
and the piper bags the air
ready for the explosion
blowing the pipe
the skirl of notes
captivates the dawn chorus
a magic interlude
to draw the breath
of the onlookers
to welcome them
to a new understanding -
riding the 'path'
we journey with them
longing for peace
longing to find that grace
longing to blend in so serenely
with our spiritual selves
and we have seen our Heaven
here, in a Suffolk Sanctuary
where the beat of our hearts
have pulsated in a cosmic
familial response
to Leonora's wisdom and love -
arigato Leonora
om shanti shanti shanti
irashaimasen

*Receiving Reiki initiation – 14th April 2002*

## THE MEADOW FAIRY

I encountered a fairy in a meadow
As I was minding my own business
Enjoying the pleasantness of a country walk
Except
I inadvertently stepped upon a wayward yellow celandine
Whose head hung over
Strayed onto uncharted, human soil
But then… such madness did I evoke within that tiny breast
The fairy's unhinged wrath
Did I experience!
She flew into a furious rage
When, rising from the depths of tall field grasses
She blew her horn against scarlet lips
She stamped her feet on an invisible platform
(Could it be cloud?)
She snatched at my spectacles
She punctured my septum with her fiery sword
And made me sneeze
Poor little soul
Thus was she drenched by peppermint droplets
Too heavy for her to hold her flight
She fell to earth like a grounded bumble bee
All heavy from the day's gathering of wild flower nectar
Shackled by his own enthusiasm
Thus did she lie shaking in a diaphanous heap
 I bent down and gently picked her up
Dried her on my cotton handkerchief

And lectured her that not all humans
Are so offensive on country walks only
It just so happened
That her celandine had been doomed
Fated to a squashing of her petals by my over-sized boots
Too big for narrow paths
We laughed then and
Shaking hands
Well, she shook my little finger
Playfully imprinting it with a mossy-green tinge
As though it were her benchmark
(Do fairies leave their essence behind on meeting with a stranger?)
I watched her as she fluttered beyond my vision
Delicate, gossamer-winged nymph
I likened her to a damselfly
But her wings were microscopic moonbeams
Compared to the dazzle of those of the dragonflies
Which flit and dart about castle ruins and other such environs
So
She must have been a fairy
After all

*For Catherine - 26 April 2002*

## FLUMMOXED

you wore
grey leggings
soft cloth
against your skin
I saw the outline
of your nakedness
I wonder what Victoria Wood
would say
if she had seen you!
Ooooh
but your tackle
looks as good
as anyone's!
thing is though
why don't you accept my love?
are men losing their ability
afraid of infertility?
or are they becoming alienated
from us?
if somebody knows the answer
please
would you tell me?

*remembering Australia 1986 : June 2002*

## NEEDS

I'm not in competition with the other poets
Only I could do with earning a bob or two
My shoes are Sophie's
My Jigsaw designer suit is Sophie's
My overcoat, 100% pure wool, is Sophie's
Auntie gave me her three-piece suite
Green, inflammable and oversized
For my living-room
William unstrapped his watch
Just for me to wear
When the motor-biker broke mine
And left me there to grieve
For my naked wrist
What do I care if everything is second-hand
The rain has shoved loose brick-dust
Down the chimney breast
Mum gave me her Dyson today
Sooty scraps on my blue carpet
Sucked up
Dancing dust trails in the empty room
Hair trapped in the brushes
Is this what life is all about?

*June 2002*

# REJECTION

Nobody wants to know me
No man wants to know me
I look in the mirror
I am past my prime
Lined
Weather-beaten
And my eyes
Talk
Rejection has been
My constant companion
So
I reject you
Before you shake my hand

*flashbacks from the car crash making one traumatised – July 2002*

# TRYING TO BE ME

in haste
I take this book
and think of another
who wanted to know me
but the only love
was the dark-haired enigma
I had no interest for outside dalliances
I wonder
am I myself?
I try to be me
but the me doesn't come out right

*more flashbacks – July 2002*

## MEMORIES

Remember
when the kids were small
remember
remember
wrong shoes on tiny feet
and parents struggling
to maintain their calm
lace Time to their elbows
tick-tock their tongues
at feisty fledglings
ripping ribbons
shredding stitches
howling without tears
remember
remember
when the kids were small?
Kookaburras serenaded us
from a Eucalyptus jungle
remember?

*August 2002*

## ARRESTED DEVELOPMENT

He plays with me
he says
come come
then his mate, Dave, calls round
and he says
go go
just like a child at play
when three's a crowd -
I won't have any more truck
from my pal with arrested development
once I loved you
and still  I do
but I had to say
Adieu
Adieu

*September 2002*

## THE PHYSIOTHERAPIST

I have to know
why
I have to know
why
I have to know
why
why did he play
'Love love me do'
his hands
manipulating the needles
burning
turning
cavorting silently
I feel him close
we talk of Robbie Burns
I cannot see his face
only the couch
through the porthole
'read to me'
I ask
half laughing
his voice gives me pleasure
the needles give me pain
yet
he has made me
(almost)
whole again

*to my physio with thanks for brilliant treatments – September 2002 – Ipswich,*
*Suffolk*

## POEM FOR ADRIAN (*February 2003*)

There's a chap wha bides in Tayport
an anither in Dundee
but they are baith my juniors
an far tae young fer me
there's a doctor doon in Boreham
wha I met the ither week
an' although he's verra handsome
I hae turned the ither cheek
then again, I luv ma angel
wha helps me soothe ma dreams
but despite oor close encounters
he does not tie up my seams
there's a laddie lives by Eastbridge
sic a tender, sweet embrace
did we share between us
till anither took ma space
so I asked  ma angel "tell me
am I far too auld, or bent?
is it true tha' ony guid fowk
their Soul Mate to them is sent?"
then a tiny birdie telt me
"Penny, wha's this a' aboot?
you don't need tae seek a lover
till yer lover seeks you oot!"
but my frien' today has asked me
"come one, tell me, do,
wha is it that you fancy?
is he Jock, or Jack or Clancy?
does he dance the Hielan' dancy?"
I have nae idea
do you??

## FOR ADRIAN FROM BOBBIE

Adrian:

"quietly she sleeps
beneath a cross of red
splashed on wintry cotton
soft cloth for her head"

Bobbie:

"I slumber
motionless as the black cat at midnight
while latent memories
casually glide
through my dormant hours

until you reappear
and taking my hand
we shall dissolve
back into the heart of God"

*Adrian's wife, Bobbie, died of ovarian cancer in September 2002.  This is a tribute to an extraordinarily courageous lady.*

## ENGLAND OUR ENGLAND

Fast flows the avenues of time,
courted by majestic cavalry, sublime
chastely resplendent on their ebony steeds
they hasten to the Royal creed
onward and over the Pennine Chain,
cantering southwards to Salisbury's Plain
and we are almost home again

A stroll past Brixton's dusty doorways
lures haunting dreams of Cornish shore ways
golden the sands of azure seas
hiding our Earth's sweet mysteries
and Dunwich bones from ancient graves
that once were men and once were slaves
speak to us like Ships of Glory
ready to expose their story

A ghostly repartee rings out
"is this what history's about?"
surely we did not die in vain?
our ashes laid in acid rain?
England, our England, there shall be
only one England
stand by me!

*competition for 'Poem for Britain', 15ᵗʰ March 2003*

41

## I AM

I am a sailing ship
I am a bird in the sky

I am a steam train

I am a shuttlecock
keeping out of the rain

I am a tortoise
I am a fish in the sea

I am an aeroplane

I am an eagle
winging to far off Spain

I am
I am
I am everything

I am everything but dead

*from my book 'Hope's Deliverance', June 2003*

## MUSES OF A BACKPACKER 1985

Is that you God
hiding beneath the Sun?
or are you the face of the Moon?
looking glum
because all we do is fight
all we do is wish for more…
what is it we are looking for?
I have the answer
tucked away in my backpack
right in the smallest corner
among the dust and the lint…
when I fly home
I shall turn the backpack inside out
and shout to the world
GOD ISN'T A TINY GRAIN OF SAND
SHUT AWAY UNTIL WE THINK WE NEED HIM
HE IS HERE! HERE! HERE! HERE!
listen
nothing is as important as
the understanding of the Universe
and
God is waiting

*from my book 'Hope's Deliverance', June 2003*

## IN A GREEN FIELD

I woke up to find that darkness called me
clear skies had been my aim, my eventual gain
but the Sorceress of Lives Past
had waved her twitch of Hazel twigs over my brow
to conjure up all manner of fearful, demonic fantasies

and in burst a million goblins
O My Soul

then great, chunky cankers formed from Nowhere
clustered beneath armpits, tender thighs, scratchy belly
my mirrored image cracked back at me
the exposure of a pathetic siren
caught in the maelstrom of her errors

and in burst a stream of Pipistrelles
O My Soul

and as scabby corms replaced one-gold hair
I stood watching since my eyes were clear
left, no doubt, to witness my own change
while the Goblins played upon my misery
and the Pipistrelles nipped at soft flesh
plucked sinews sent notes of shame careering into the air

there
O My Soul
I grounded
in a green field                    *July 2003*

## SISTERS

she stood at the top of the stairs
laughing in high-pitched tones -
the five year old with the fractured grin
had pushed her sibling sister
and watched her
bump
bump
bump
tumbling like a rag doll
all the way
to the bottom stair
where the child
grabbed the rail
and held on tight
then
looking up
grinned at her wayward sister
as if to say
'I may be smaller than you
but
I shall always be
one step ahead...'

*August 2003*

## DIAMONDS

diamonds
sparkled out
their story
cut from
mines
earthed
and languishing
while countless feet
trod the soil above them
then
the star appeared
and shone
her charismatic coils of light
onto a sleeping babe
Christ was born
and the diamonds
spun
crystal paths
to synchronise
with all
that was
Holy

*Christmas 2004*

# CONTEMPLATION

I leant on Dunnottar Castle's field-stile
lingering by the ruin's entrance
watching fat sheep on green hillocks
waddle
their fluffing woollen fleeces
swinging
like greatcoats in the wind
this way
that way
shifting their heaviness
behind the gusting air
carrying their unborn lambs
a caravan of innocents
preparing for the birth journey
and I think of Prestonpans
as Jonnie Cope's men
slept
while Charlie's boys
crept in for the slaughter

*May 2005 : commended in the 2006 Crabbe Memorial Poetry Competition,*
*Suffolk*

## THE MUSTANG

the mustang
sniffed the air
held her head
snaffling at the bit
while the lion watched
knowing
when the bridle
was hanging from the arm
of the man in spurs
and cold beer
sent aromatic pungencies
on cool draughts
of evening air
then the mustang
was her bait

but the mustang
followed behind
the weary cowboy
shoed hoofs
covering
flattened footprints
on dusty trail
and whinnied
over the stable door
while the lion
slunk back
empty-mouthed
to her hungry cubs

*22 May 2005*

## BREATH

breath calls me
ragged ripples in stagnant waters
I hear the alarum of bells
I feel the beestings of needles
I smell the watery blood
I see the waxed patina of my skin

breath calls me
and the burrowing of a drill
sucking, sucking, sucking out my life substance
while the man in white
tells me, kindly,
'you have leukaemia'

I have six days before the light goes out

breath calls me
easier now, I am infused with transfused blood
I 'see' the donor's face
a bonny girl
with large, spread-eagled hands
she gives me life

breath calls me
it is one hundred and six days past the flickering light
and I can walk your path

*March 2006*

## THE CHASE

I was walking through a field of corn
when the SNAP of a rat's teeth
drew blood

from my left side, drip, drip, drip
then the SNIFF of a canine's muzzle
sent breath-waves

down into the furthest recess of my lungs
while the dog PUSHED hard with his slimy nose,
leaving imprints

of ruddy incisors on wrinkled skin –
thus was FEAR invited into my soul
to say – for a day or so

yet the dream does not release its anguish….

*12 May 2006, after a nightmare*

## LOST IN LOUGHTON

blue jag - fat bloke at the wheel -
tail-gating my mazda in a 30 mile limit
while I kept an eagle watch for signs -
'Chigwell' spied on small white post
followed the arrow
only to end at a crossroads
which way to take?
took a chance and turned towards the new road
ended up at Sainsbury's car park
hooted at by irate shoppers
(tell the man who gave me the two-bit finger signal
hope he ends up a pig in a poke)
drove noseward uphill past the industrial estate
left at the lights and back where I'd begun -
and there - a silent image in the 6 foot skyline -
the scuffed letters of 'Theydon Bois'
breathing out my safety line
the signpost man had raised an arm in salutation
he must have had a vision of a lady lost in Loughton -
and all I wanted was to find my way back home

*27 June 2007*

## RICH PICKIN'S

'how old are you?' the young man said
pulling at his hoody
'how old are you, with your bright red lips
and your face all moody!'

'why' said I 'I am an old old soul
from the nebula en grace
'and where is that?' he asked in awe
'are you from another race?'

'why, no, young man, we're all the same
just different ways of thinkin'...

I placed inside his palm a silver coin
the 'gypsy's' sensitive perception
'seeing' the man he soon would be -
but now the child with hungry eyes
playing a wicked game
of who beats who
of how much he could bleed
from the lady with a fat purse
but all I had was a silver coin -

he turned away
and laughing
looked back and called
'thanks lady! rich pickins!'

*8 October 2007*

## LIMERICKS

*some fun for the ladies of the Tewel WRI,*
*Aberdeenshire, 2007*

There wis an auld mannie fae Skye
Who saw that the larder'd run dry
"Wife! Go kill the goose
Or ye're oot o' this hoose!
An' nae a tear will there be in my eye!"

There once was a poet called Burns
Whose life was a series of turns
A legend in time
His words and his rhyme
Have brought much joy to the Mearns

There was a rural Wifie fae Tewel
Who owned an ass of a mule
Each time that she rode
This donkey – he crowed
"Fill me up fer I'm empty o' fuel!"

There was a Rural Wifie fae Tewel
Who did high kicks fae her 3-legged stool
Her foot hit the door
An' she fair hit the floor
Crying "Help ma boab I'm a silly auld fool!"

There was a Rural Wifie fae Tewel
Who yelled at her husband "You fool!
The hen's in the pot
An' the fox ate the lot
Ye can ne'er turn the neeps intae gruel!"

## A BROKEN VASE

I broke a vase
on Christmas Day
sitting on a floor cushion
pulling at flowers
bound up with string

nobody told me off
because of my
stupidity
this family who have learned
the language of laughter

graced me with
gentle smiles
while the chef said
'leave it to me'
and cleared up all the splinters

*London, Christmas Day, 25th December 2007*

## THE MASK

you were watching me
observing my reaction
as we discussed the Japanese
and their wearing of the mask
to protect the outside world
from the virulence of a cold
and the impact of their sneeze
upon unsuspecting innocents

then you exclaimed
'and what is behind your mask!'
a breeze of shock sent sparks
into the latent atmosphere
and trembling, I disposed of the
dishes at the sink, waiting to be dried
and found a new voice
at first, thready and weak

but then, rallied by a spiritual strength
I found the courage to respond
'be happy inside yourself, my friend!'
contentment is a gentle thought
a listening ear, a smile, a word of encouragement
as with those who meditate and look within
so their success glows
and the light burns with the force of grace

*3rd January 2008*

## THE MAN WITH THE HAT

Mexican Sombrero
bonnet from France
bowler on a City head
a cap saying 'Vodaphone'
all travelling along the New Cross Road

but it is Jamaica Jim's Stetson
precariously perched
in contrast to the ankled hemline
of his overcoat
that tells a story

of a blues man walking the city streets
his feet stepping like drumbeats
pacing in time with the trundling, thundering
traffic, exhausts blasting a gaseous tribute
to the days when soul sang out their message

'yeah baby
love is the way'

*4th January 2008*

## IN DAYS GONE BY

In days gone by
when you and I were nothing but a dream
weaving in and out of two lovers' kisses

In days gone by
when steam trains hissed their coal smoke
over green hills splashed by morning glories

In days gone by
when horses whinnied at the whip
pulling carts wedged between heavy shafts

Miss Sahara lived in her oasis
full-water springs quenched the thirst of wild beasts at rest
and languid jungle trees stood tall and graceful

Happy in their rain-soaked hey-days
blessed by the harmony of birdsong
mossy river banks
cricket calls
macaques at play
as the eyes of the lynx
peering from behind the far mountains
kept her secrets

In days gone by
mother Orang-utan gurgled at her baby
not behind iron bars
but from the freedom of her rain forests -
untouched and dignified

*10th January 2008*

## CHILDHOOD

She was walking
Between two high hedges
Their leaves flustering
In a warm breeze
Whipped from fields of corn

When all at once
She saw tall beech trees
Nodding to her
In richly spoken welcome
Inviting her to join the party

But she did not know
Did not see the bull
Who cursed all newcomers
Who traversed his field
Where his family dwelt

And as she tripped over the grass
She heard the snort
Saw the breath cloud
Transported from his nasal passages
Giving her a chance to RUN!

The old bull knew, you see,
Knew she was just a young human child
So he too tripped and capered
Across his field
Holding back until the child was safe

She breathed gallons of white breath
As she stood gasping
On the other side of the fence
And realising she had made
A new friend…

With a wave of delight
She left the herd behind
Looking for a soft spot
In which to deliberate
On all that was happening in her life –

Then, seeing a tunnel opening
She crawled into the thicket
For some yards, because
There, in the middle of the gorse
Was the most beautiful flower she had ever seen..

An orchid, purple and proud
Had found its home
Away from trampling feet
Away from children's fingers
Only now to be discovered…

But the child loved all nature
And sitting down beside the flower
She began to sing a silent song
Thanking her new found friends
For cherishing her in this supreme
    wilderness

Sleep overcame her
Only to be woken by the sound of barking
And the whirr of a saw on wood
So - softly she left that special place
And returned home in joyous contemplation

That child was me
In 1955…..

*21 October 2015*

## EXISTENCE

When the world is silver
And the seas turn gold

*When the skies are water*
*No more to hold*

Clouds of darkness
Nor streams of blood

*And Noah returns*
*Upon the flood*

 Then we are born
As rainbow ochres -

*No colour difference*
*no statistical players*
*no politicians*
*no soothsayers*
*no incriminating looks*
*no wars*
*no soldiers*
*no police states*
*no landlocked borders*

Just the Law of Innocence
And the World
At Peace

*7 August 2011*

## THIS WONDERFUL WORLD

This wonderful world
I watch the white slashes of gulls
queuing like children in line
wings beating
beaks prodding
pulling fat worms
from the newly ploughed field beyond

this wonderful world
I listen to the stillness of the night
while bats sweep and glide
black shadows
an eerie contrast
slammed against the backdrop
of the harvest moon

this wonderful world
I hear the lowing of the cows
at milking time
their heavy udders
giving way
to the suck-suck-sucking
of the milking machines

this wonderful world
I close my eyes and feel
the calmness of the sea yonder
just over the hill from where I sit

while grey seals bathe and slide
over the rocky outcrops
dark silken stumps
piercing the waters
as the pools empty and fill –
empty and fill
in motion
with the ebb and flow
of the moon tide

this wonderful world
we can never match her offerings

nor recognise her sufferings –
this wonderful world
she it is
who gives us
all that we need

*Dunnottar Braes, Stonehaven, October 2007*